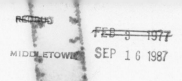

j301.42 Naylor, Phyllis
N   Reynolds

Getting along i
your family

35253 000

Getting Along
in Your Family

GETTING ALONG IN YOUR FAMILY

PHYLLIS REYNOLDS NAYLOR

Drawings By
Rick Cooley

ABINGDON   NASHVILLE

GETTING ALONG IN YOUR FAMILY

Library of Congress Cataloging in Publication Data

NAYLOR, PHYLLIS REYNOLDS.
    Getting along in your family.
    Includes bibliographical references.
    SUMMARY: A handbook of psychological principles for getting along
in a family. Includes such topics as fair treatment, loyalty, divorce,
sharing tasks, and fighting.
    1. Family—Juvenile literature. 2. Parent and child—Juvenile litera-
ture. 3. Brothers and sisters—Juvenile literature. 4. Problem family—
Juvenile literature.
    [1. Family life] I. Cooley, Rick. II. Title.
HQ734.N37   301.42′7   75-44295

ISBN 0-687-14120-6

To Jeffrey and Michael
who, without knowing, helped write this book

CONTENTS

Getting Along
in Your Family

WHAT'S A
FAMILY FOR?

To have breakfast with. To celebrate Thanksgiving with. To visit Grandmother with. To go shopping with. To fuss with, laugh with, fight with, feel with. A family is for sharing things together in a caring kind of way.

Many families have a mother, father, and several children. But not all. Some have seven children, and some have none. Some families are without a mother, some without a father, and some have grandparents, cousins, uncles, or aunts living with them.

Sometimes two families come together to make one. When a divorced or widowed parent of one family marries a divorced or widowed parent of another, each often brings children of the first marriage into the new one, and suddenly there are brothers and sisters all over the place.

Parents who adopt their children can sometimes choose a boy or girl with black or blond hair. But most people do not get a choice as to what their children will be like, and, of course, no one asks the baby's opinion at all.

Some babies are lucky about the family they get. Some are not. It's all a matter of chance, and there are no refunds or exchanges.

Think what it would be like to have been born a spider or a salmon and to have entered life without a sign of parents anywhere. Or to have been a turtle egg and been gobbled up by a snake when you were less than a minute old. But you weren't. You belong with a family of people, and you will be with them for quite a few years before you are ready to go out on your own.

Probably most of the time you are glad that you're all living together. But other times you wonder why there has to be such a thing as a family at all. You're sure you could do quite well without a brat of a brother and sauerkraut for supper and all the other things that go along with a house full of people.

Families have been around a long time—as far back as history goes. We know of no society that has managed very long without them. The family has developed into one of the best ways to take care of the children. When a child was born, the mother nursed it and kept it warm while the father went out to find food. The woman knew that she could count on the man to bring home food and also animal skins to keep her warm. The man knew that he could count on the woman to cook the meat for him and to make the furs into clothing. The woman knew that the man would return home each day, and the man knew that she would be waiting for him when he did. It was important that they could depend on each other. Together they taught their children the things which they had learned, and when the children were grown, they, in turn, looked for mates with whom they could live and start their own families.

It is nice to live with people who share our interests and care about us—people we can count on. It is fun to be a part of a group that enjoys doing things together. But most of all, a family is important because all of its members know that each one in it is special to all the rest—that what happens to each concerns the others very much.

Then why is there so much fuss in the family sometimes? Why don't people who love each other get along better? What can kids do with the kind of family they've got?

That's what this book is about.

CHAPTER 1

EVERYBODY
HAS A PROBLEM

WHO'S THE LUCKIEST?

Have you ever wished that you had been born first? Or last? Just think what you would be able to do if you were the oldest child in your family, and what you could get away with if you were the youngest! Or what about being the middle child? She doesn't have to do any of the hard work because she's not old enough, yet she never has to be in bed by seven like the youngest.

No matter how many children there are in a family, at some time or other each of them thinks it's someone else who has the best deal. David,

Alan, and Mark are twelve, ten, and seven. At least half his waking hours, Alan, the middle child, envies David, the oldest. David stays up till midnight sometimes. He's always doing fascinating things such as building an electric engine or collecting stuff to look at under his microscope. He gets the largest allowance, and Dad brags about him to relatives. Alan feels sure that David is his parents' favorite.

David, however, believes that Mark, the youngest, is the pet of the family. According to David, Mark gets out of doing work whenever he wants. All he has to do is whine, "Aw, that's too hard for me," and Mother or Father finds someone else to do it. There's even a difference in his parents' voices when they talk to Mark—more gentle, more patient. And whenever there's a quarrel, no matter who started it, it seems Mark never gets scolded as much as the others do.

If seven-year-old Mark had his choice, however, he'd rather be Alan. Alan can go off by himself for an hour and nobody even notices. Whenever their parents go out, they seem to leave instructions for David and rules for Mark, but they never say anything about what Alan has to do. Alan, because he's in the middle, can do just about whatever he likes and nobody bothers him.

In a way, all three boys are right. There definitely are advantages to being the oldest, the youngest, or the middle child. There are advantages to being parents instead of children, too. But there are also disadvantages.

Though David arrived in the family first and had his parents all to himself for the first two years—admired by relatives and paraded in front of friends—David has his own special set of problems. Because he is the oldest, he is expected to have more self-control and better judgment than his brothers. If all three boys get into mischief, David often gets the blame "because he should have known better." His parents want him to set a good example for Alan and Mark by getting along well with his teachers at school and showing responsibility around the house. David remembers the arguments he had with his parents before they finally allowed him to stay up till nine-thirty on school nights. Now Alan is still running around at ten o'clock most

evenings, and Mom and Dad don't think anything about it. "You guys don't know how easy
you have it!" David tells his brothers. "I'm the
one who always has to fight the first round, not
you."

Mark, however, at age seven, doesn't have it
easy either. It seems that no matter how many
birthdays he has, his parents still look upon him
as their baby. David and Alan can go anywhere
they like on their bikes, but Mark is limited to
six blocks. David has all kinds of secrets, and
Alan belongs to a club, but Mark is too young to
join. Mark isn't allowed in the community pool
unless he has somebody older with him. Nobody
wants him on their team when the kids play
baseball, and he still has trouble with his shoe
laces. When David tells a joke at the dinner
table, everyone laughs. When Mark makes one
up, everybody groans, and Alan says, "Ha . . . Ha
. . . Ha," without even smiling.

But Alan, too, has problems. It's true that he
could disappear for an hour and nobody would
miss him, but that's part of the trouble. David
gets special attention because he is the oldest,
and when Mark manages to do something new,

it's always a big deal because he's youngest. Sometimes it seems that their parents overlook all the things that are special about Alan, and he wishes that they would praise him even half as much as they seem to do David and Mark.

The fact is that parents do not love all their children in the same way. When Dad wants to show Mark affection, he grabs him and gives him a big hug. When he is feeling loving toward Alan, he usually hand-wrestles with him awhile, something Alan particularly enjoys. And when he is especially fond of David, he shows it in his eyes—a special way of smiling. Or he might put one hand on David's shoulder, shake him a little, and say, "You're a pretty good guy, you know it?"

Boys and girls sometimes think that the affection a parent shows another child means that that child is loved more. It's good to remember that we wouldn't really want to be loved in exactly the same ways as our brothers and sisters. David, Alan, and Mark would not really be happy if their mother treated each of them exactly the same—if she assigned each of them exactly the same jobs and gave each a quick kiss on the left cheek before he left for school in the morning. Each boy wants to know that he is special in some way.

David might like to hear her say, "Good luck on that science project, David; I know how hard you've been working on it." Alan might like her to ask if his ankle is feeling any better since he sprained it, and Mark might like her assurance that she'll leave some cookies on the table for him when he gets home.

Sometimes people in small families think that everything would be fine if theirs were a larger family. The chores would be divided up, the older ones could help the younger with homework, and there might even be enough kids in one house to make up a basketball team. At the same time, children with six or seven brothers and sisters often envy those with only one or two. If there weren't so many children in their family, there would be more money for other things. They each could have a room of his or her own, and they could go on a real vacation and afford to stay in motels and eat at restaurants like many other people.

It's so easy to look at another person or

another family and see only the advantages. But everyone has problems, even parents.

PARENTS ARE PEOPLE TOO

When you were a baby, your parents probably seemed the most powerful people in the world. If you were wet, your parents made you dry. If you were hungry or cold or hot, they made you full or warm or cool. Even as you grew older, your parents seemed able to do anything. They knew how to get money and buy groceries, to read a road map and drive a car, to catch a bus, wash the clothes, bake a cake, fix a bicycle, paint the walls, and call the doctor on the telephone. They filled out all kinds of important looking papers, got lots of mail, planted tomatoes, called the plumber, and made sense out of all the confusion on the first day of school.

Parents, you might have thought, were simply big people whose job it was to take care of you. They were awake when you got up in the morning and saw that you were properly dressed and fed before you went to school. Chances are that even if your mother worked at an outside job, she was there when you came home in the afternoon, eager to hear all about your day. You probably felt that your parents were for listening to your problems, buying your clothes, fixing your breakfast, repairing your toys, taking you to the doctor, and spending all their waking hours thinking up things for you to do.

Of course this just isn't true. No matter how much parents love their children, they think about other things too. If you had never been born, your parents would still have lives of their own and other interests to keep them busy.

Just because a man is forty years old and weighs a hundred and eighty pounds doesn't mean that he is never frightened or worried or even childish. Just because a woman is thirty-five and has three children doesn't mean she doesn't feel pain when she goes to the dentist or that she enjoys doing the income tax or never misses her own mother. Parents, too, feel lonely sometimes, or angry. They may not cry as often or kick a chair when they are mad, but they have feelings which are just as real as yours and worries that often have nothing to do with you.

Parents make mistakes. They do or say foolish

things which embarrass them. Sometimes they are uncomfortable about meeting strangers. They may worry about whether they are doing good work on their jobs and what the boss thinks about them. Sometimes they have problems getting along with the neighbors. They may argue with the plumber, or perhaps they feel bad because they believe someone has cheated them. They can be upset when the car won't start or disappointed because a relative is making a nuisance of himself. All sorts of things go on every day in a parent's thoughts that children don't know about.

Sometimes problems get all mixed up, and it's hard to tell which is whose. Bob's mother married again, and Bob found himself with a new eight-year-old sister named Janet. As if it weren't hard enough getting used to a girl around the house, Bob did not feel very comfortable with his new father either. Mr. Jacobs liked things to be orderly and quiet. He was not used to the way Bob played his phonograph or the fact that Bob left his sneakers just inside the front door. When Mr. Jacobs came home in the evenings, he would call Bob right away to pick up his shoes and turn the phonograph down.

Bob's mother, however, had problems too. She did not always get along well with Janet. Janet seemed to feel that only her father could tell her what to do, and she was slow to obey her new mother—if at all. There were problems at meal times, because no one seemed to like the same foods; and since both parents worked until five, Bob and Janet would often spend their after-school hours teasing each other and arguing. The evening would be miserable for all of them. There were good times too, of course—times when Bob almost felt he loved his new family—but they all wondered just why it was they couldn't get along better.

Fortunately, most family problems gradually work themselves out. Somewhere along the line one family member finds a way to solve his own particular problem so that he doesn't pass his grumpiness along to someone else. But sometimes little problems are allowed to grow and grow until the whole family is tangled up, and then it may take hard work to get out of the web.

A SAFE PLACE FOR FEELINGS

A home should be a place where we are able to show others what we are feeling. If we enjoy something, we can share it with other people. If we are sad, we are able to ask for comfort. When we feel loving, we can express it with a hug or compliment without feeling embarrassed or awkward. We can be kind to others without wisecracks and teasing.

Whenever people are living together, however, disagreements arise about the way to do things. A happy family is not one which has no problems but one in which each person knows it is safe to bring out feelings. These may be angry feelings or sad feelings; and while the others may not always agree, at least they accept the way that person feels and try to understand.

Unhappy families have a difficult time doing this. Often they *want* to work out their problems, but they just don't know how, or things are so tangled up it is hard to know where to begin. Some families feel that children shouldn't disagree with their parents, or that parents should never disagree with each other. They may be shocked when somebody gets really angry—as though a person has no right to feel this way. Sometimes the most unhappy people are those who never quarrel at all but keep their feelings hidden, not only from each other, but from themselves.

A home should be a place where every member can really be himself. This does not mean that everyone can do just as he likes. It does not mean that Richard can throw a book through the window because he is angry or that Suzanne can call her parents names. But Richard should be able to say, "I *feel* like tearing the house down when you do that to me!" or Suzanne to say, "I *hate* it when you scold me in front of company!" or John can say, "I'm *afraid* to go to the pool alone and need someone to go with me."

If angry words make your parents uncomfortable, perhaps you could tell them how important it is for you to show how you feel. If they do not like the way you've chosen, maybe together you can work out some other way.

A home should be a safe place for feelings.

CHAPTER 2

LIVING WITH LOVE

ENJOYING EACH OTHER

If everyone in your family were exactly alike, you would probably all be bored silly. If one person played the violin, you'd all play the violin. If one of you liked creamed chicken, you'd all eat it, and if someone got grumpy when the weather was bad, you'd all sit around glaring at each other every time it rained.

Fortunately, most families aren't like this. Though all the people in a family may be alike in some ways, they are very different in others. They may all happen to have red hair and like banana pie, but at the same time each one has unique qualities. One may like to read mystery books more than anything else; another would rather play soccer. One's favorite subject is math; somebody else prefers music. Even though the family lives together in the same house, each member is a separate, unique person.

People who get along well together respect each other's differences. But respect means more than just putting up with somebody else—it means actually enjoying that person and that person's differences.

Kevin's family consists of himself and his parents. They tolerate each other's differences, but they do not respect them. Kevin is a stamp collector, and spends long hours looking over his catalogs. Kevin's mother does not understand this. She is a person who likes to have people around, and it annoys her that Kevin spends so much time alone. When she passes the door of his room and sees him working on his stamps, she usually sighs and says somewhat disgustedly, "I see you're going to spend the day doing *that* again!" She doesn't make him stop, but she obviously doesn't like it.

Kevin, meanwhile, thinks that his parents' activities are stupid. He thinks it's silly that his father spends his Saturdays playing golf. (Only a numbskull could enjoy hitting a little ball around all day.) And the same goes for his mother's garden club.

Lori, her brother, and her mother make up Lori's family. Each of them is as different from the other as rain and sunshine. Mrs. Wells is an artist with an advertising firm. On weekends she likes to paint and make mobiles or sculptures. John, Lori's brother, is in high school and wants to become a newspaper reporter. He once drew a picture of the three little pigs, and everyone thought they were chickens. He hasn't drawn a picture since; and whenever the family needs a laugh, John brings out that old picture, and they all howl over it together.

On the other hand, John's mother is so poor at letter writing that she leaves this to her son, and it is John who drops a note to Grandma each week. Lori doesn't know what she's good at yet. Sometimes she enjoys making things out of wire and clay or writing make-believe stories. But most of the time she is dreaming about the horse she wishes she could have; and, knowing how important this is to her, Mrs. Wells is going to enroll her in riding classes in the fall.

John and Lori enjoy each new painting or mobile their mother makes, even though this often takes up weekend time that she could be spending with them. And Lori and her mother look forward to reading the school newspaper that John edits. This family not only tolerates their differences, but enjoys them as well. Their lives are richer because they can share their talents.

Sure, you say, it's easy to respect the good things about someone else. But how about the other things? How do you enjoy a sister who's so slow that you could run around the block twice in the time it takes her to put her shoes on? Or a little brother who's so afraid of dogs that he can't go outside if there's a puppy in sight? How do you enjoy a mother who's still working on her master's degree and is studying most of the time, or a dad who has the basement cluttered with things he's started but never finished?

Have you ever seen a family get together and talk about the good times they've had? Chances are, the things they thought were so much fun did not seem quite so funny when they happened, but looking back on it, a family sees the humor and remembers it fondly. The morning they were on their way to church and ran out of gas because Dad forgot to fill the tank—as usual—will be one of the memories they laugh about together for years. The fact that they had to walk the rest of the way in the rain wasn't very funny at the time, but it is funny thinking about it now. The way Dad forgets to do things becomes just one of the characteristics that make him different from the others.

It's actually possible to enjoy a mom who is a part-time student. It's possible to enjoy a sister who is slow—to enjoy her relaxed, carefree way of moving around and doing things. It is possible to feel real affection for a brother who runs at the sight of a puppy and to make a game out of guessing what Dad's working on now and when he will get it finished, if ever. If Dad didn't have three projects going at once he just wouldn't be Dad, would he? And if Martha were not so slow that she's still on her cereal when you leave for school, she just wouldn't be Martha. Of course there are some habits and characteristics which aren't funny in any sense of the word and never will be; but these are far fewer than we think.

Much as we hate to admit it, there are things about ourselves, too, that others don't particularly care for. Our own habits are so natural to us, they don't really seem so bad. And so it is with Dad and Mom and Martha and Benjy.

BEING LOYAL

It makes sense that of all the people in the world, you care about yourself most—or certainly as much as anyone else. After all, who else is going to brush your teeth, put you to bed when you're tired, cry when you stub your toe, and make sure you get that second dish of ice cream?

It's your job to take good care of yourself. As you grow older, however, you will learn to care about some of the people close to you as much as you care for yourself.

Families sometimes feel close together outside the home but separate inside it. Some children like to talk about "our vacation" and "our dad" and "our way of doing things" but lose their team spirit once they walk inside the front door. In some homes, everyone is so busy looking out for himself that it doesn't seem much like a family at all but rather a group at an auction all bidding against each other.

In even the happiest families, there are little jealousies that flare up now and then. But sometimes children seem to be constantly on the lookout lest someone else get a bigger piece of cake or the prize in the cereal box. Boys and girls often have really vicious arguments about who has to turn off the TV or who set the table last. Jealousy among children can become so intense that a mother will actually find herself measuring the juice she is pouring or the pie she is cutting to convince her children that they are getting equal shares. Parents, too, may behave like rivals. As if forgetting that they married because they loved each other, they may argue over who has to work the hardest or who drove the kids to their swimming lessons last week.

Sometimes, the individuals in a family seem loyal to no one but themselves.

Loyalty means having love and concern for the people in your family in good times and bad and never talking about them behind their backs or saying things that could injure their feelings or their reputations.

Being loyal means not hurting or embarrassing your family unnecessarily. It means looking out for each other's safety and happiness. It means trusting each other and proving that you are a person who can be depended upon.

There are certain things that should not be talked about outside the family except to certain people whose job it is to help with problems. We don't tell our friends and neighbors everything we know about our families, not because the things are bad but because some of them are very personal and nobody's business except yours and your family's.

You may be ten years old and still sleep with your teddy bear. That's all right (and it's nobody's business but yours), yet you might be embarrassed if your brother told his friends. Perhaps your sister was punished at school for talking too much. Perhaps you know that your mother has false teeth or you know why your father's first marriage didn't work out. These are things you should keep secret unless your family says that you may tell someone.

Loyal people keep their word. If a boy tells his mother he will pick up his baby sister at nursery school and care for her till his mother gets home from work, it means that he will be there on time. It does not mean picking the baby up half an hour late or bringing a bunch of friends home with him. A loyal person does not laugh at the expense of another. Being swell to a brother at home and then making jokes about him to one's friend is not being loyal. Parents show loyalty, too. A loyal parent does not listen to his children's secrets or fears and then tell them to the neighbors.

HOW TO SHOW LOVE

Being loyal is part of being loving. A loyal family *knows* that its members love each other. They feel it and show it and say it. For some, this comes as easy as breathing.

Some people find it far easier to fight than to

love. They *want* to express the way they feel, they *want* to be close, but there are so many problems or fears that keep them from being loving that they fight instead.

If it has always been hard for you to show affection for someone, it may take a little practice, but you can learn how. To begin, you will have to get rid of all the reasons why you don't show affection.

Erica and her sister Debbie played together on a baseball team. During the last game of the season Debbie played poorly, and the team lost. Though the two girls seemed to quarrel more often than not, Erica felt very sorry for her sister that day. Somehow she wanted to let Debbie know that she understood how badly she must feel, that she still liked her regardless of what the rest of the players said. She thought of saying something nice to her, but each time she stopped because of what she expected Debbie might answer. Perhaps her sister would say: "Lot of good that does me;" or, "Oh, leave me alone. Who cares what you think?" or "You didn't play so well yourself."

Whenever we think of saying or doing something nice, we can always think of a dozen reasons why we shouldn't. If we let these reasons get in the way of loving and rarely show the good feelings we have toward others, we can hardly expect them to feel very loving toward us. If someone responds bitterly or impolitely to our offer of help or love, that is that person's problem, not ours. And perhaps the next time we try it, he or she will have thought it over and will respond better.

How many times during the day or week do you think something good about people without telling them?

Have you ever admired your little brother's ingenuity without telling him how clever he was? Played a game of table tennis with your dad (when you knew he was tired) without thanking him afterwards for playing with you? Realized that your sister looked especially attractive on a particular day but resisted telling her so?

Do you ever feel like giving your parents a quick hug but don't? Feel like sympathizing with your mother when she has worked hard all day but don't say anything? Feel like saying, "I really like you because . . ." to someone in your family but remain quiet?

What keeps us from showing love? Perhaps we think that the other person already knows how we feel. That may be so, but everyone likes hearing it said. Do we ever get tired of hearing people tell us that they enjoy having us around or they think we have a great sense of humor or they're glad we're part of the family?

Perhaps we feel embarrassed; we think we'll be laughed at. Or we worry that someone will say something mean in return. Love means taking chances. It means risking it three or four times, perhaps, before the other person responds. But *somebody* has to take the first step. No family got to be loving without working at it.

Sometimes we don't have as much trouble *showing* love as we do accepting it from others, strange as this seems. Sometimes people may express love in a way we don't like.

If Stephanie had her choice, her mother would say things to her like, "Stephie, you're great. I don't think I could have wished for a better daughter." Or, "You're a nice gal to have around, you know it?" Instead, when Stephanie's mother is feeling affectionate, she grabs her daughter and kisses her just as she did when Stephanie was two. When Stephanie does something her father thinks is good, he says, "Chip off the old block." When Ken, her older brother, feels good toward her, he grabs her ankles as she goes up the stairs or swats her with the newspaper. And Stephanie's younger sister shows her admiration by following her around all day.

But that's how love is. We all show it in our own way. Stephanie can, if she likes, push away from her mother. She can tell her father he is merely bragging about himself when he calls her a "chip off the old block." She can yell at Ken to stop teasing her and tell her little sister to mind her own business. But if Stephanie is looking for love, she will take her family as they are and accept their love in the ways they show it best.

Parents sometimes show affection in ways that are difficult to understand. These are not always the best ways either; but perhaps they are the only ones they know. Mothers and fathers who were raised in homes where their parents did not show love easily, where there were few hugs or kisses, may feel uncomfortable about being warm and loving in their own homes. Perhaps they don't even realize how much more loving they could be. One mother may show love by cooking delicious meals and giving a lot of attention to food. She may buy her children candy when they perform well in school or after they have just had a painful visit to the doctor. For some reason she finds it easier to give a candy bar than to tell her children that she is proud of them or to offer them sympathy when they are hurt. Perhaps she is a mother who shows love and concern by worrying all the time about her children's health or safety.

Some fathers find it easier to give money than to show love more openly. When they are feeling affectionate or proud or sympathetic toward a son or daughter, they hand them a dollar bill instead of saying the kind words their children would like to hear; they just can't seem to get the words out or don't know they need to be said.

Yet just as our parents accepted us when we came into the family as babies—whether we were cute or ugly, skinny or fat, fussy or good-tempered—we, too, must accept them and their own faults. And if they cannot show us easily that they love us, there is no law which says we can't show them how we feel and no reason why we can't hug them. And perhaps if they see how easy it is for us, they will try it themselves.

NO MAGIC, JUST WORK

Happy families don't just happen, they are made—by lots of effort and patience. Just wishing won't do it.

Some of the ways of working at it are really very simple.

When someone in the family is in a bad mood, it makes sense to stay out of the way until he or she feels better. People who are very upset or angry or tense are in no condition to listen to someone else. Instead, they want others to understand them, and at that moment they are not especially concerned about how others may feel.

Jim was building a tree house in the backyard. He had spent most of the morning on it, and just when he thought he had the floor in tight, one side tipped, sending him sprawling to the branch below and scraping his leg. He climbed down and threw his hammer on the ground in anger.

Clyde, his stepbrother, watched him for a moment and said, "Boy, I know how you feel. Those things are hard to build."

Jim didn't answer, but he felt that at least someone understood. And after he'd sat down with a soda pop and glared at the tree house for awhile, he asked his brother's help, and the two went off to work on it together.

Clyde didn't have to say what he did. He could have yelled, "I *told* you the left side was tipping, dummy! Some tree house!" And Jim would probably have jumped him; they would have rolled all over the porch kicking and punching; and Dad would have sent them to their rooms for the rest of the afternoon.

How do you know what to say when someone else is feeling grumpy? Sometimes saying nothing is better than saying the wrong thing. With a little practice, however, you can learn to put yourself in another's shoes—to say to yourself, "How would I feel if I'd worked all morning on the tree house and then it fell down? What would I want somebody to say to me?"

If you're in a bad mood yourself, give your family some warning. Don't make them find out the hard way. When the teacher scolds you and you lose your best ballpoint pen and it rains when you were going to play outdoors, it helps if, when you walk in the house, you call out, "I'm in a rotten mood, everybody, so better lay low." You may get a few remarks and some quizzical looks, but your family will probably take you at your word and be pretty cautious with you till you feel better.

Everybody has a right to privacy. People are entitled to be alone with their feelings for a while without anyone interfering. Brothers and sisters, mothers and fathers, we, ourselves, are all entitled to have thoughts that we do not have to share unless we want to, a place where we can go to be alone, and conversations or letters which we may keep private. Sometimes it is hard for parents to understand that children have this right and that they do not have to know everything a child is thinking. And sometimes it is hard for children to understand that parents are also entitled to private conversations or periods of time in which they want to be alone together, away from their children.

One secret of getting along well is not to make a fuss over unimportant things. You'd be surprised how many families have a real ruckus because someone ate all the ice cream or says he likes one football team better than another.

Getting along means giving the people in your family the same consideration you'd give your best friend. Do you ever compliment your friends but never think to tell your mother what a good dinner she made? Do you rush to a friend's house when the friend has a problem but never take time to comfort a brother or sister? Many tell their friends all about their various plans, how they are doing in school, and what happened at the party but seldom share these things with their parents unless they are asked.

A loving family shares their lives. They let

one another know how they are feeling and what they are doing and where they are going, not just because they should, but because they want to. Anger, when it is shared, becomes less bitter; sadness becomes more bearable; and happiness is increased many times over.

CHAPTER 3

HOW TO
FIGHT "POLITE"

PICKING THE TIME AND PLACE

No matter how much you may love your parents or your brothers and sisters, there are times when you are angry at them—furious, in fact. Boys and girls need a chance to show how they feel, and parents need to let off steam as well. But whether your arguments will lead to shouting matches or solutions depends a lot on how you go about it.

There are rules for discussing touchy subjects and fighting, just as there are rules for getting along together. When some people are angry, they can, by what they say, swing and lop off a head in one blow. This gets the tension over in a hurry, but if you win the argument and lose your best friend, you haven't gained a thing.

Other people aren't quite so bold about their feelings. They pick up the ax and chop away a little at a time—a word here, a look there, a nasty remark now and then—but they never really speak up and get their feelings out in the open. They make everyone, including themselves, thoroughly miserable.

And some people aren't even brave enough to hack away. They mutter and mumble and end up with headaches or stomach pains; for by shutting up their feelings in this way, their anger is turned against themselves.

If you want a really good free-for-all that gets things out in the open and accomplishes something, you've got to choose your time and place carefully. If you expect any kind of victory at all, you're not going to argue with your sister about whose turn it is to vacuum right after she's fallen downstairs and cut her lip. The worst time in the world to ask for a raise in your allowance is when your father is rushing to get to work on time. And if you wait till your mother is balancing the checkbook to ask for one good reason why you can't have the gang over that evening, she'll give you a dozen.

As to picking the place, try to keep your arguments private. If you've got to have it out with your younger brother because he keeps using your colored pencils without permission, wait till he's alone—don't embarrass him in front of his friends. If you walk in on your mother when she's chatting with some neighbors and announce that the sandwiches she's been putting in your lunch are lousy, she probably won't say much then, but she'll certainly remember how you've embarrassed her.

When two people are having an argument, it's best for others to stay out of it. If your father is scolding your sister for not helping enough around the house, it doesn't help for you to chip in with even more examples of what she has not done. It's not fighting fair to gang up on somebody who is already down.

CHOOSING WEAPONS

Some people, when they quarrel, are not actually trying to settle anything. All they really want to do is hurt each other.

If you are so furious that all you want to do is
say the meanest, most unkind thing possible,
then you'll pick the deadliest, sharpest words
you know. You will look for the sore spots in the
other person, all his private little faults, and jab
away at these. If your dad insists on taking a
short cut to the stadium and succeeds in getting
to the game late, you'll remind him of all the
other times he's goofed up, tell him he never
could read a map, and remark that he's getting
old. If your sister's overweight and has done
something to make you angry, you'll call her a
fat creep. You will have scored your point, all
right; your sword will have gone right to the
heart. But it may be a long time before you feel
the two of you are friends again. It is tempting to
want to hurt someone who has hurt you, but it is
far better to try to bring about a constructive
change than to cause injury or embarrassment.

Don't exaggerate. If your mother is sometimes
late picking you up at school to take you to
music lessons, don't yell, "You *always* get me
there late!" To tell her that you've been late
three times in the past month is sobering

enough. If your brother isn't as generous as you are, don't say, "You *never* want to share anything." Just reminding him that you shared your chocolate bar with him twice recently brings home the point.

Your job, when you disagree, is to say what *you* think and feel, not to guess why the other person does what she does or to call her names. If your little brother has been raiding your chewing gum supply, stick to how *you* feel about it. Say, "It makes me boiling mad to walk in here and find that you've been in my drawer again." Don't say, "You're nothing but a low-down thief!" If your father has a way of losing his temper and then trying to make up for it later by passing out quarters, don't say, "Yeah, you're always trying to buy us off after you make a big scene." It's much more helpful to say, "I can use the quarter, Dad, but I'd much rather you didn't lose your temper in the first place."

It may seem to you that only a very wise person would be able to say just the right thing at the right time. But if you remember to stick to how *you* feel and how the problem affects *you* instead of focusing on the other person and calling names, you will probably say the right thing most of the time.

When you are arguing, keep to the subject. If you and your sister are quarreling about how long she talks on the phone, don't start in about how she embarrasses you at school too. Save that for another day. If you both keep bringing up all the things you can think of, the argument could last a month, and you'd never resolve the telephone problem.

Try to keep your feelings out in the open and be honest about what they are. If you have been hurt or embarrassed, say so—if not right then, certainly later. The reason for disagreeing at all is to show exactly how you feel so that something can be done. People won't make the effort to change unless they know what your feelings are. Some people start a fight and then sit on it. They never say exactly what is bothering them. Some people, in fact, have such a hard time talking about how they feel that they just walk around all day with their lower lip stuck out, and the family has to guess what is wrong. Was it something that happened yesterday or this morning? Was it because Mom spoke too sharply or because Dad threw out the comic section?

If your sister has worn your blouses three mornings in a row, and you're fed up with it, don't say, "I suppose you're going to raid my closet again today." Come right out with it and say, "Look, Marcie, I'm tired of you taking my clothes. Iron a blouse of your own to wear." If your father keeps calling you a pet name he used when you were a baby, don't clam up and scowl every time he does it. Say, "Dad, I'm too old for that now, and it makes me angry when you keep calling me that."

It never helps to keep anger or jealousy or sadness locked up, because these feelings will either eat away at you, making you miserable, or escape a little at a time, making others miserable—even people you don't mean to hurt.

A GOOD QUARREL

Sometimes we act as though the person we are quarreling with is deaf, blind, and an idiot as well. We shout, stamp our feet, and pound the table to make our point. Such behavior may make us feel better, but it will hardly convince

the other person that we have something
worthwhile to say.

If you want to be persuasive with your
parents, calmly give them intelligent reasons for
wanting what you do or for objecting to what it
is they want. Don't say, "Only a creep would
wear a pair of shoes like that." Tell them why
you don't like the shoes they think you should
buy: the tops are so high that they'll make your
feet sweat; the soles are so slick that you'll slip at
recess; or, simply, they hurt.

If you can, give them a choice. Tell them
you'll be glad to wear brown leather shoes to
school this fall if they can find a pair with crepe
soles.

Whatever you do, don't make threats. They
may prove embarrassing. If you threaten to run
away unless you get what you want, your dad
may very well hand you your suitcase and call
your bluff. At the very least, it will convince
your parents that you are still behaving like a
small child. Threats are a poor way to deal with
anybody. It is far better that a person give in
because he feels your argument is reasonable
than because he or she has been bullied.

It's amazing how often we argue without really understanding what the other person says. We are so busy thinking of what we will say next that we don't listen carefully to the other point of view. Try as best you can to see the other person's side, even though you believe he is wrong.

Let's say that you have a brother Stevie, and the two of you have an agreement that one week he gets the prize in the cereal box and the next week you do. Last week he got it, and now it's your turn. But today he's crying and says he wants this week's prize as well.

Some older sisters, in a case like this, would pound Stevie on the shoulder, grab the prize, and leave him crying in the kitchen. But if they really made the effort to listen to what Stevie is saying, they would understand how he feels. Most of the prizes which he got so far, Stevie is sobbing, were too hard for him to put together, and he could never play with them. You were able to work all your prizes because you're older. This particular prize, however, needs no putting together, so he feels he should have it to make up for the others.

Now the problem isn't quite so simple. An agreement was made, it's true, and according to the agreement, it's your turn for the prize. But in some ways the agreement wasn't quite fair, though neither of you realized it at the time. And perhaps a sister who really wanted to be fair about it would decide on some sort of solution. Perhaps she would volunteer to put some of those other prizes together for Stevie. Perhaps she would offer to give Stevie the new prize once she was through playing with it. Or perhaps she would suggest that the family buy the same cereal next week so that Stevie could have one of his own.

It is important to think ahead. "What will happen if I say this?" is a good question to ask yourself. Or, "What will happen if I don't?"

If you say nothing at all, is the irritation so small that you can honestly forget about it? Or underneath will you feel a little angry for a while? If you blurt out how you feel, can you trust yourself to attack the problem, not the person? Even when you can't give in to what other people want, it helps to let them know that you're trying to understand how they feel.

When you've tracked mud over the floor your big brother has just scrubbed and he is yelling at you about it, you *can* say, "Okay, so I made a mistake! Didn't you ever make one?" and chances are he'll go on yelling. Or you can say, "I'm sorry, Bob. I know this really makes a lot of work for you," and the yelling will undoubtedly stop. You can even offer to clean up the floor, and that's best of all.

What follows is a typical argument handled differently in two different homes. In the first, Danny gets back from a friend's house later than he'd promised.

Mrs. Evans: You're late getting home, Danny.

Danny: A lousy twenty minutes, that's all.

Mr. Evans: It wouldn't make any difference if it were only two minutes, young man. You said nine o'clock, and that's when we expected you.

Danny: Two minutes! Boy, you're just trying to

make trouble! Nobody in his right mind
would make a fuss over two minutes!

Mrs. Evans: The point is, you've been late the
last three times you've gone out, and you
promised you'd be back on time this evening.

Danny: So, we were playing a game over at Ed's,
and the time just slipped up on me. You'd
think I did it on purpose or something!

Mr. Evans: Well, we're going to have to put a
stop to this. We'll take those twenty minutes
off tomorrow night. You'll have to be home at
8:40.

Danny: Tomorrow night! Boy, you've just been
waiting to ruin Friday night, haven't you? Just
waiting!

Mrs. Evans: What's so special about tomorrow
night?

Danny: If you've forgotten, just skip it. You
never remember things that are important to
me.

Mr. Evans: Well, are you going to tell us or not?

Danny: I'm not going to tell you any more about
my life than I have to. What's the use?

Mr. Evans: Okay, you've had your chance. If you
won't discuss it, neither will we. Twenty

minutes earlier tomorrow night, and that's final.

Danny: Don't worry. I'll be here. Whatever you say, Sergeant. Just wait till I'm eighteen. I can't wait to get out of this place.

In the second home, Pete also gets home twenty minutes late.

Mrs. Miller: You're late getting home, Peter.

Pete: Only twenty minutes.

Mr. Miller: It wouldn't have made any difference if it were only two minutes. You said nine o'clock, and that's when we expected you.

Pete: I'm sorry, but Ed and I got interested in a game at his house and I just forgot about the time. I didn't do it on purpose.

Mr. Miller: Well, this has happened the last three times you've gone out, and it's got to stop. We'll take twenty minutes off tomorrow's curfew, so you'll have to be home by 8:40 instead of nine.

Pete: Eight-forty! Tomorrow night! Gee whizz, Dad, not *tomorrow* night!

Mrs. Miller: What's so special about tomorrow?

Pete: Have you forgotten?

Mrs. Miller: I guess we have.

Pete: Doug's having a birthday party and his folks are taking all the guys bowling. I've been waiting and waiting for this party. How can I ask his dad to drive me home right in the middle of it?

Mr. Miller: Okay. I tell you what. We'll take the twenty minutes off the following night instead. But if you're late then, you can't go out the next day at all. Fair enough?

Pete: I guess so—if you really think that twenty minutes is worth punishing.

Mr. Miller: It is, Pete, when it gets to be a habit. When you show us that we can count on your getting home on time, maybe we'll make the curfew nine-thirty. But you've got to prove to us that you can take the responsibility. Agreed?

Pete: Okay, agreed.

PET PEEVES

Every family has them—long lists of things that make them angry. Sometimes parents' lists all sound surprisingly alike, and so do the children's. They all wonder why the others can't

see things from their point of view once in a while. It is important to figure out where the trouble that leads to constant arguments lies and to try to work out a system that stops arguments from happening. Here is a list of things which children and parents frequently argue about, as seen from both sides of the fence.

NOISE:
   Children: "Maybe sometimes we do get a little loud, but our parents complain about things like just laughing out loud or calling each other or bouncing a ball on the bedroom floor. They've had forty years to practice talking softly, and they don't realize that we're just being natural. We're younger, that's all. They expect us to act like old folks."
   Parents: "Sometimes the noise in this house gets so bad that our heads really ache. We'll be enjoying a quiet meal after the children leave the table, and suddenly there's an earsplitting shriek in the hallway or someone jumps down a half-flight of stairs or the front door bangs. The children *know* the noise is coming: they know when they're going to shriek or bang a door, and

their nervous systems are prepared for it. But it takes us by surprise and sends shock waves through us. It really makes us angry."

ROUGH PLAY:

Children: "We could understand their griping if we played football inside or roller-skated in the hallway or something, but most of the time they yell when we're just wrestling a little on the rug or crawling around on the bunk beds. They act like we're trying to kill each other."

Parents: "It's true that a lot of the time we tell them to stop when they're not doing anything particularly bad just then. But we know from experience that rough play tends to get wilder and wilder and may get completely out of hand. It makes us nervous listening to the yells and thuds, knowing that at any minute someone is going to get hurt or tip over a lamp or something. The kids just don't seem to know when to stop."

FOOD:

Children: "Tastes are different. They get angry when we don't like something that they do and keep on telling us that it's good. Well, maybe it's good to them but not to us. I'll bet they didn't like it either when they were our age. We won't starve if we don't eat everything on our plates."

Parents: "It makes us angry to spend money on food and an hour or more cooking it and then have the kids come to the table and turn up their noses before they even taste it. If they had their way, we'd eat hamburger and spaghetti every night of the week. They don't realize that there was a time they didn't like pizza either, but they learned to like it. They should at least take a few bites of everything."

QUARRELING:

Children: "Our parents yell at us before they even know what we're quarreling about. Half the time they don't even wait to find out who started the fight; they simply punish us both."

Parents: "How do you decide who started a quarrel when each insists the other was at fault? Whom do you believe? Our kids quarrel over anything, no matter how silly. You name it, they'll fuss about it."

NAGGING:

Children: "The thing about parents is they talk too much. They tell you to do something, and five minutes later they tell you again. Or else they give you a long lecture on why something has to be done instead of saying it in a few words. They should just tell us once and get it over with."

Parents: "Believe us, there's nothing we'd like more than to tell the children once what has to be done and then forget it. They say they'll do something, but they don't. If we don't keep reminding them to do their homework or get ready for school, they'd never get their assignments done and would miss the bus half the time."

KNOWING WHAT TO EXPECT

In getting along with other people, it's important that we know what to expect from them, and they from us. If there is a rule against wrestling in the living room, boys and girls get confused if sometimes they are punished for it and sometimes they are not.

It's the same with brothers and sisters. If part

of the time you let your small brother turn somersaults on your bed and then suddenly get angry with him and tell him to stop, he doesn't know what to expect.

People who live together should be able to count on each other not to change too much from day to day.

When two families come together to form a new one, it is especially important that feelings stay out in the open so that everyone has some idea of what to expect. You have lived with the members of your first family so long that you just assume they know all about you—what you like and dislike—even though this may not be true. But new brothers and sisters or fathers and mothers may not know much about you at all. They may expect you to act or feel or think as they do and be surprised to discover that you react differently. They may be used to a lot of good-natured teasing among themselves, for example, and cannot understand why teasing upsets you.

Some families speak in naturally loud voices, others are soft spoken. Some are very neat, others leave things lying around, and it does not seem to bother them. Some families like to have friends around much of the time; others prefer living more to themselves. When fathers and mothers from two families marry, some of their ways of living may be very different. Usually they have talked these things over and decided that they can be happy in spite of their differences, but the children may find it far more difficult. It is very easy for the children of each family to think that their own way of doing things is the best or right way simply because they are used to it.

Another problem is that children often act as though they don't have to obey the new adult in the family. When Kitty's divorced mother married a man named Bill, Kitty refused to do anything he asked.

"My father never made me go to the drugstore for him," she would say. "Why don't you go buy a newspaper yourself?"

And John, whose father married again, would say, "My mother doesn't care if I put my feet on her couch."

It is especially difficult if you live in one home during the week and another on weekends or during vacations. Each household has its own way of doing things and its own rules.

"My father says I can do anything I want!" some children say when scolded by a new parent. But if you really want to get along and make your home a happy place for everyone, you will follow the rules in each house, however different they might be.

Getting used to each other can be a big problem or an adventure. Usually it is a little of both. The stepbrothers and sisters and step-fathers and mothers who look forward to sharing their lives, to learning about the habits and interests of the new members of their family, will probably find that more people mean more fun, because what's more fun than a happy family?

CHAPTER 4

DECIDING WHAT'S BEST

WHOSE JOB IS IT?

Some families, it's sad to say, fuss all the time about whose turn it is to do something, whose job it is, whose responsibility, and so on. They never sit down and talk it out but go on month after month, year after year, arguing. The spirit of the home seems to be competition instead of cooperation.

Part of the problem is that families have changed a lot since your grandparents and great-grandparents were small. Back then it was probably more simple. The father's job was to earn the money for his family, to feed the horses, harvest the crops, and take care of the big chores and the outside work. The mother's job was to take care of everything inside the house— preserving the food, cooking, cleaning, and sewing. The boys helped their father in the barn, the girls helped their mother in the house, and that was that.

Today it is not so simple. In many families both the mother and father work outside the home. Both come home tired at the end of the day, yet there is still dinner to make and household chores to be done. Although most fathers weren't taught to do housework when they were young, it is neither fair nor possible for a working mother to do it all.

When a family tries to solve this problem with love and understanding, they usually find a solution. There are any number of ways to divide up the work, with all the family members doing the job they do best. In some homes, the father spends more time with the children than the mother does, or perhaps he does most of the cooking. It doesn't matter at all as long as the arrangement works out for that particular household.

When a family begins to divide up the work, there are all sorts of questions to be considered. Who works the longest hours? Who gets home from work or school first? Who is the last to leave the house in the morning? Who has lessons after school or meetings or part-time jobs?

Some families get stuck on the wrong kind of questions. They let unimportant things determine what work each one should do. The mother and father may argue about which of them earns the most money, deciding that this person shouldn't have to do any housework. Some boys and girls argue over what is "boy's work" or "girl's work" instead of trying to divide things up fairly between them.

Everyone can take on responsibilities around the house. Even the youngest can put his own toys away. Five-year-olds can empty waste baskets, pick up trash in the yard, and do many small tasks that others took care of before.

Older brothers and sisters can help with the vacuuming, dust the furniture, and scrub the bathtub. A young teen-ager can wash windows, make lunch, and help with the laundry and shopping. Children of all ages can help rake leaves, shovel snow, and wash the car.

Some families find it helpful to post a list of daily chores for family members, changing it each year as the children grow older. In one family, the children are expected to do their daily jobs before they leave for school in the morning. And because they want to come home to an afternoon free for play, they are glad to get their work out of the way.

Knowing ahead of time what jobs are to be done and when they should be completed means that the parents do not have to nag about them or interrupt a child when he is busy doing something else. Such a plan seems to work out well for everyone in the family, as long as the children show that they are independent enough to get their work done.

Rules are important. It may seem sometimes that things would be better if everyone just did what he thought was best, but actually life wouldn't be very pleasant at all. If a rule seems unfair, however, tell your parents why you think

so. Choose a time when they are not worrying about other things and suggest how the rule might be changed. It always seems to help if, instead of just criticizing, you offer something better.

There are times when one person has to take over the work of another. Perhaps the mother is ill, and the father and children must cook and do the laundry for several weeks or longer. Perhaps there are financial problems, and the mother and older children have to take jobs to help pay the expenses. When a new baby comes into the family, older brothers and sisters often have to help care for it in addition to their other duties. When one brother goes to summer camp, the other may be expected to do his work while he is away. In a loving family, each person is willing to help the others, do more than his own share, and change the rules to fit the situation. That's the way it is with loving.

FAIR OR NOT?

One way of deciding what is best for a family is to take into consideration what is fair to each of its members. It's not always easy to know exactly what is fair and what is not. In some situations there are several possible solutions. What would you suggest for the following common problems?

Christine was watching TV when her brother threw a sofa pillow at her.

"Stop it!" she snapped.

"Stop it!" Charlie mimicked.

Christine picked up the pillow and threw it back. It missed and hit the piano keys instead.

"Cut out the noise down there!" Father yelled.

"Ha, ha! Missed me!" Charlie whispered.

Christine picked up a magazine this time and aimed it. It hit Charlie on the side of the face. He threw it back and it hit Christine over the eye, making a small cut. Christine shrieked.

Father came downstairs and turned off the TV.

"Daddy!" Christine cried. "I was watching my favorite program. Charlie started the whole thing!"

"I said to stop the noise and you kids didn't," Father boomed. "Both of you go to your rooms till I say you can come out."

Fair or not?

Mother discovered Joseph crying, and after she quieted him down, she learned that Joseph had traded his best racing car to Timothy for some candy, and now he wanted it back.

"He agreed to do it!" Timothy protested when Mother asked him about it. "It's not my fault if he made a bad bargain. He ate my candy, and now he wants his car back. Tough luck!"

"Joseph's not old enough to understand what's a good bargain and what's not, but you are," Mother replied.

"Then he'll just have to learn the hard way," said Timothy. "He traded it to me, and now it's mine."

Fair or not?

Gloria and Connie were only a year apart, but they seemed miles apart in getting along with each other. One day Gloria went into Connie's room to borrow her dictionary. In getting it down from the shelf, she accidentally knocked off a clay bowl which Connie had made in art class. Connie heard the crash and came running upstairs to find the bowl in pieces on the floor.

In a fury, she rushed into Gloria's room and

broke one of the miniature dolls in her collection.

Fair or not?

Father had warned the boys not to play football in the backyard.

"You can pass it, but you can't kick it," he said. "If you do, and break a window, you'll have to pay for it. Take it to the school ground instead."

For a few days Billy and Paul stuck to simply passing the ball, but after a while they began kicking it again, and one day Paul sent it flying through the dining room window.

Mr. Edgars was angry when he came home. He sent Paul to his room to get money from his bank to pay for it, and when Saturday came, set to work to fix it.

It was a long, tiring job, too difficult for either Billy or Paul to do. The slivers of glass had to be carefully removed, piece by piece from the window frame and the new pane puttied in place. It took Father most of the afternoon, a day he had hoped to play chess instead. Paul had paid for the window pane, but still it was Father who had to do the work. And so, for as long as Father worked on the window, Paul had to sit on a chair as punishment.

Fair or not?

When Sherry's father married again, he chose a wife who already had a small daughter. Sherry didn't mind taking her new sister with her when she went to the movies, the swimming pool, or the playground on Saturdays. But one day a friend asked Sherry over for the evening with some other fourth-grade girls. They were going to make costumes for the school play. Sherry's new mother asked her to take Jo Ann too. Sherry wanted to get along with her new mother, but this was too much.

"Mother!" Sherry cried. "Marie didn't invite Jo Ann. There aren't going to be any other little kids there."

"She won't be in the way," Mother said. "She doesn't have as many friends as you, and I don't think it would hurt to take her along and let her watch."

"Nobody else has to take her little sister everywhere she goes," Sherry insisted. "Pretty soon they won't invite me at all if they know that Jo Ann's coming along."

Fair or not?

Peter and Kenny were raking leaves and had been promised ten cents for each sack they filled. Nine-year-old Peter seemed to handle the rake well, but six-year-old Kenny had a more difficult time. Consequently, Peter was filling sacks much faster than Kenny. When it came time to be paid, Peter claimed that they shouldn't get the same amount of money.

"I'll bet I filled most of those bags myself," he complained. "You should pay me for the ones I did and pay Kenny for the ones he did."

"No!" Kenny cried. "I've been working just as long as Peter has. It's not my fault if I'm slower."

Fair or not?

Jimmy thought that once he reached the sixth grade, things would be different. Mother had been working at the library till five-thirty each day since he was in third grade, and Jimmy was used to coming home from school and amusing himself till she got home. By the time he was in fourth grade, he wished he could sometimes ask a friend to come in and play Monopoly or something, but Mother said, "No friends," unless an adult were in the house. The same thing happened in fifth grade. If he wanted to play with friends he had to go to their homes. Some of the other mothers worked and weren't home either, but none of the other boys got into trouble. Most of the time the boys simply played cards at the table or watched TV. Now he had reached sixth grade, and when he asked his mother if this year he could invite friends in, she said the same thing: "No friends till I get home."

Fair or not?

Nancy had a rather quick temper. When things were going badly for her, she became so angry that she sometimes threw her pillow across the room, knocked over her chair, banged her door, or ripped the pictures off her bulletin board.

One day she had been working very hard in the yard weeding for her parents. She was hot and tired. As she came into the house to get a cold drink, she tripped and hurt her knee on the back steps. When she opened the refrigerator to get a Coke, she discovered they were all gone. She was so furious at all the bad luck she was having that she banged the refrigerator door as hard as she could. She banged it with such force that a plastic shelf on the inside of the door broke off. Nancy said it wasn't really her fault because everything was going wrong, and she was so angry she couldn't help it. Father said she was responsible for what she did, even when she was angry, and would have to pay the eleven dollars needed to buy a new shelf.

Fair or not?

What can you do about it if you feel that you are being treated unfairly? First make very sure that you are right. Perhaps you broke a rule, but you feel you should go unpunished this time for some reason. If you want your parents to make an exception in your case, ask yourself if this would be unfair to anyone else. If your sister or brother were in a similar situation, would you want your parents to make an exception for them? If you still feel that you are being treated unfairly, explain it to your parents and suggest a better way. They may not agree, but it's better to take that chance than to keep your feelings hidden. And they might decide later that you were right and think twice if the same situation comes up again.

MONEY PROBLEMS

It sometimes seems as though a home would be a happier place if it weren't for that five-letter word MONEY. Many families argue about money more than anything else. Yet there are wealthy people in beautiful houses who are not really loved by anyone, and there are families living in tin-roofed shacks who love and enjoy one another. Money can make our lives easier, but not necessarily any happier. Some families don't argue much about money at all. How do they manage?

The home is a good place to learn how to save money and also how to spend it wisely. Some parents give a weekly allowance to their children. Others pay a certain amount for each chore about the house, and the child gets paid according to how much work he or she does. Whatever works out best for your family is what you should do, remembering, however, that much of the work we do in life is done simply because it needs doing or because we want to please someone, and thus it goes unpaid. If you are not yet receiving money of your own, perhaps you could discuss this with your parents. Ask their suggestions as to how you might begin to have experience with money.

Many children think that they should receive a bigger allowance simply because their friends do. How much you receive depends partly on how much your parents can afford and how much you are expected to buy with it. If you are supposed to buy your lunch at school, pay for your music lessons, or purchase some of your own clothes, you will naturally need more than if your allowance is spent only on popcorn, ice cream, and comic books. One eleven-year-old boy who is allowed to spend his allowance any way he likes divides it into three parts: 10 percent goes into a special bank account toward his college education; 40 percent goes to buy stamps for his collection; 20 percent is put aside to buy Christmas and birthday presents for his family; and the rest is spent on ice cream and other treats.

If you spend all your allowance in one day and your parents give you more money to last out the week, you don't really learn anything about budgeting your money. When you are grown, you cannot go to the boss for more money if you have spent all your paycheck two days after you've received it, so now is a good time to learn to save and spend wisely. When you buy a cheap toy that breaks right away, you will look at toys more carefully in the future before you buy them. When you give your money to friends or spend it all in one day, you will feel sorry later in the week when you discover you haven't any left to buy ice cream after school. It is from mistakes like these that we learn to be more careful, however.

It's hard to believe, but you would probably be far less happy if you had everything you wanted. Many children think that if they could have every toy, book, or record that they wished, they would be happy. But that's not really true; they would be bored. Half the pleasure comes from wanting something so badly that you can hardly sleep at night; dreaming about it, working for it, planning for it, talking about it, being afraid you might not get it, and then earning enough money to buy it after all, or even finding it under the tree on Christmas morning.

If you *knew* it would be under your tree—if you knew that your parents would buy whatever you want—it wouldn't be nearly as much fun, would it?

CHAPTER 5

WHEN TROUBLES ARE TERRIBLE

PROBLEMS: HOW THEY BEGIN

It is true that most of the things we worry about never happen, and that problems have a way of working out all right. But sometimes a family comes up against a really big trouble. These troubles can start from outside the home or come from within.

Problems that come from outside can, but don't always, draw the parents and children closer together. The problem becomes an enemy, and the family works together to fight it. It might be a problem with a neighborhood that is too dirty or noisy or unsafe. Or perhaps the parents' jobs do not pay enough to buy all the food and clothes which the family needs, and in sharing with each other, the family members feel closer. Perhaps the father is hurt in an accident. Loving families stand by each other, even when troubles are awful.

When troubles come from within the family, however, they are often more difficult to live with. A father who drinks too much or a mother who is mentally ill or a brother who is in trouble with the law or parents who fight all the time make it very hard for the rest of the family.

When people are causing a lot of trouble, it is hard to remember the good things about them. But the brother or sister who is the most difficult to get along with may actually be the one who needs love and praise the most. And the parent who drinks may be the one who is the most miserable inside. People especially need support when they have failed in something that was important to them.

A person who seems to hate others is unhappy with himself. When things are going badly for us, we often strike out at others. A father who has had a rough time on the job may be particularly grouchy with his family. A girl who has quarreled with her best friend may come home and push her baby brother out of the way. Most people are like this at times.

But when people face more serious troubles that stay with them a long time—possibly troubles inside themselves—their unhappiness may cause them to mistreat their families. Sometimes the mistreatment is in the form of words. A parent may constantly say things to embarrass or ridicule the children, to make them feel stupid or ugly or unlovable. Sometimes the mistreatment consists of actions that don't harm physically, but still injure. A boy may be forced to take care of his small brothers and sisters each day after school until midnight while his mother works, and on weekends, as well, while she goes out to parties. He may never be allowed to invite in friends of his own or to do any of the things for fun that other children do. Or perhaps the mistreatment is physical. Parents with violent tempers have been known to burn their children with cigarettes or to break their arms. Just as there are children who sometimes torture small helpless animals, there are adults who do the same to their children. It also happens that a parent will mistreat his or her children one day and be very sorry about it the next, yet mistreat them again the following week.

Why can't these parents be stopped? They can, but somebody has to be told about it first. And there are many parts to the problem.

Some parents never hit their children, some spank them occasionally, some beat them, and a few injure them seriously. A parent who never hits or spanks may believe that kindness works best in helping a child learn right from wrong. A parent who is very strict may believe that harsh, swift punishment works best. What is considered a severe punishment in one home may not seem very bad at all in another.

In all states, however, there are laws against child abuse. Every girl and boy has the right to a home in which he or she is not physically injured, locked up, or sexually molested. If a child has physical injuries, he has been punished too severely, and there are laws against this. If something like this is happening in your family, you do not have to accept it just because you are a child.

WHO CAN HELP

The welfare department in your community wants not only to protect children from violent parents, but to help find out why the parents behave that way and to help them work out their problems. Whenever possible, they try to keep the family together. If they feel that a child's life is in danger, however, or that the parents will almost certainly injure the child as before, they may place the children in foster homes for a while. In most cases, however, this does not happen.

If you have been severely hurt by a parent, you will first need to be treated at the hospital emergency room; the doctors there will get in touch with your local welfare department which will, in turn, begin working with your parents to see what can be done about their problems.

If you have not been hurt that seriously, but have still been beaten by a parent and are afraid to stay at home, it is best to go to a sympathetic neighbor or relative and ask them to take you in for a few hours or days. Perhaps some of them already know about the situation in your home and would like very much to help you in some way.

If you need immediate help and there are no relatives or neighbors to whom you can turn, then you should call or go to the police. They will see that you are protected and will contact the local welfare department.

What if the situation isn't quite that serious and your life is not in danger? It may be an alcoholic father who storms through the house, breaking furniture, or a mother who is depressed and sits at home all day with the shades drawn, crying. It may be parents who fight all the time and threaten each other, or a brother or sister on drugs. If there are no relatives living near you, and all the neighbors work and are too busy to get involved, whom can you talk to about problems in your home?

Teachers usually know a lot about problems like these because they work with so many children. Ask your teacher if you can talk with him or her alone after school. Some children are afraid to admit that things are going badly at home for fear their teachers will think less of them somehow. This is not true, because teachers know that your parents' behavior tells about them, not you, and besides, your teachers have probably already guessed that you were worried about something. Children who are miserable at home show it in many different ways, and teachers are pretty observant. So are school counselors, nurses, principals, and Sunday school teachers.

If you look around, in fact, there are many people who can help. The family doctor may already know about some of your family's problems. So might your minister, priest, or rabbi. Scout leaders and YMCA instructors can often find help for various problems, and librarians can tell you about organizations which you could call.

There are organizations whose job it is to help people with problems. There are even organizations to help the relatives of these people. Alcoholics Anonymous is for those who have drinking problems. Alanon is for the husbands or wives of drinkers, Alateen is for the teen-age sons and daughters of alcoholics, and some communities have organizations for children under twelve whose parents drink. Each of these

groups gets together to talk about their particular problems, to share experiences, and to offer
support and encouragement.

Gamblers Anonymous is for people who are
compulsive gamblers; Recovery, Inc. is for those
who have had serious mental disorders. There
are many programs under many different names
to treat people with drug problems. Many cities
have a family service agency or a legal aid
society in addition to the local welfare department; if you want to call them yourself and have
trouble finding the phone number, ask your
librarian or a neighbor to help you.

In addition to kind neighbors and caring
relatives, interested teachers and understanding
ministers, there are special people whose job it
is to help persons with problems. They have
worked with many different kinds of troubles,
including problems like those in your home.
School counselors are just such people. So are
psychologists, psychiatrists, and social workers.
These are men and women who have been
trained to help people talk about their real
feelings and to understand why they behave as
they do. Sometimes they see one member of the

family alone, sometimes they work with the
family as a group. When a boy or girl has
difficulties at home, it is usually a family
problem, and everyone is somehow involved.

What will happen if you or a concerned
neighbor calls the local welfare department and
asks for help?
It is not possible to say for sure because
welfare departments vary from place to place.
Some counties have many social workers avail-
able to help, some have only a few. But you
might expect something like this: a social
worker, or case worker, would come to your
home and talk with you, your parents, and your
brothers and sisters in a friendly, concerned
way. Perhaps the social worker alone could help
by making regular visits and talking things over
or by suggesting another trained person who
could be of even more help.
These professional people have the ability to
talk about problems without scolding or making
a person feel embarrassed. They are able to
listen calmly to what is said without becoming
upset—no matter how angry or unreasonable the

speaker may be. They try to be fair, listening without taking sides, and they don't allow one person to take advantage of another just because he or she is older or speaks louder or becomes angry. At the same time, they try to bring out everybody's feelings so that there is nothing left hidden or unsaid that will cause trouble later. Often, when all the feelings are out in the open and each of the family members knows how the others feel, they can go about solving the problems themselves.

Though it may seem that just talking couldn't help, talking can change a lot. Once we do not feel so weighted down with feelings we can't express, once we know that someone else cares and that we are not awful people just because we sometimes have awful thoughts, we begin to see ourselves and others more clearly. And when we begin to feel more confident of ourselves, more loved and appreciated, we can concentrate on those around us and have love left over to give to them.

Sometimes the most difficult part of solving a serious problem is making the decision to get help. Some feel that family problems are too personal to discuss with anyone else, even people who are trained to do so. Others feel that they should be able to solve the problems themselves, even though they haven't been able to do so. Some feel they can't afford to spend the money or the time to get help. But once the decision is made that a problem needs special outside help, it is a big step toward finding a solution.

LOOKING AHEAD

Often when a family is going through a very difficult time, it's pretty gloomy around the house, and a boy or girl may feel that things are even worse than they really are. It is helpful to remember that while something may be very wrong in your home, not everything is wrong. While there may be some things about your father or your mother which you truly dislike, they both have good qualities, too, which are often overlooked when the bad ones seem to take over.

Though family problems may be very serious and make you feel overwhelmed with anger or sadness or worry, you will not always feel this way. Truly you won't. No matter how awful the trouble seems, there will be good times when you will be enjoying things with your friends. The problem may not work out exactly as you'd like. You may feel sad when you think about it, but you will not think about it all the time.

Sometimes we wish so badly that we could do something about someone else's problem that we begin to think it's our responsibility. Many children feel this way when their parents quarrel—especially if the parents eventually divorce.

Doug's father moved out a year ago, and even though it was explained to him that his parents were unable to get along together, Doug wonders if he had anything to do with the divorce. He keeps remembering the times his father scolded him, the times he made a lot of noise when his father wanted it quiet, the time he broke his father's tennis racket, and the way he used to complain at the dinner table. He wonders if his father might have stayed if he hadn't been so naughty.

Fathers and mothers do not divorce because their children misbehave. It is because they have problems with each other and inside themselves, and they feel things will be better if they live apart. This is sad for everyone, but it is not the children's fault that it happens, and often things are better when the parents are not together to quarrel so much.

It is hard to sit by helplessly when two people you love are being angry at each other. The only thing a boy or girl can do when parents quarrel is to try not to make any trouble that would further upset them and to remain friendly and kind to them both.

It is hard, too, to grow up in a home where the parents are not people you want to be like. It is difficult to grow up without a model of the kind of person you admire. But fortunately, the world is full of people of all kinds, and children can often find models from among other adults they meet. Most of us, in fact, choose qualities from several different people we have admired and grow up copying those things without even realizing it. A boy may play a musical instrument because he always admired an uncle who played the trombone. When he starts a job, he may always stick with it till it's done, something he learned from his Scoutmaster. A girl may be planning a career in math because she always loved an aunt who became an accountant. All of us resemble in some ways many other people.

Good lives can be built out of all kinds of experiences. It is not the things which happen to us that are so important, but what we do about them.

Gwen's mother, for example, was an alcoholic. The worst days were school days. She seemed to start drinking from the moment Gwen's father went to work on Monday morning and then on and off all week. On Saturdays she felt guilty about neglecting her family and was extra nice for a day or two, but on Monday it happened all over again. Life was very tense for Gwen and her father and sisters. Sometimes, when Gwen was careless or forgetful or got into arguments with her sisters, her father would say, "You're going to grow up to be just like your mother."

Gwen knew it would be easy to believe that and not even try to make something of her life. The teachers and neighbors knew about her mother's problem, and perhaps everyone would say, "Well, what can you expect, after all?" But Gwen refused to let her mother's problem become her own. The worse things got at home, the harder Gwen worked to make friends with the girls at school, to get along with her teachers, and to get her homework done. She found that the more she tried, the more people reached out to help, to be friendly in return. And the better she felt about herself, the easier it made things at home with her father and sisters.

No matter what we face, there is someone somewhere who has faced it too and come out on top. No matter how difficult the problem, there is someone who can help us see it through. Families can have really awful troubles yet come through them stronger and closer than ever. A little bit of love goes a long way, and even though it may not solve the problem, it shows the rest of the family that we're trying, and perhaps they'll try a little harder too.

Love, in fact, goes on and on. Keith was only twelve when his father died, and for a while Keith didn't feel he would ever be happy again. It made him actually sick to see other boys laughing or playing ball, because the day his father died, the world seemed to turn gray, and he couldn't understand how anybody anywhere could be happy.

As the weeks went by, however, Keith learned something about death. Even though his father was no longer present, the feelings they had for each other remained. When someone teased Keith because he was so skinny, he remembered the day his slim father had put his arm around him and said, "We just come from a long line of thin people, Keith, and every one of them was smart, so don't let it bother you." And they'd laughed together. When he earned his first merit badge in Scouts, he knew exactly how proud his dad would have been of him, and just knowing this made him feel good inside. Sometimes when he was having trouble with a mischievous younger brother, he asked himself, "How would Dad have handled this?" And then he did and said the things he thought his father would have done and said and worked the problem through. Even though his dad was gone, the love stayed on, and Keith realized he wasn't as alone as he had thought.

WHAT IT'S ALL ABOUT

What is love, anyway? It is not something you can hold in your hand, but something you feel, something you show, something you give. It is not something that just happens to you; it does not fall on your family like rain. It is something which you make yourselves, and you keep it alive by giving it, taking it, sharing it, enjoying it. Mostly it is giving.

Love brings out the best in each person. A family which shows warmth and sympathy wants all of its members to be the very best persons they can possibly become. Because individual family members feel good about

106

themselves, they feel happy when something good happens to other persons in the family. They know that when they themselves succeed at something, the others will be just as proud of them and will want to help in any way they can.

There is no ideal family, however, no ideal parent, no ideal son or daughter. People are never exactly like we might wish them to be. Even warm, happy families that support each other have flare-ups occasionally, but because they know the value of getting along together, they make a special effort to work the problem through.

We can go through life angry at ourselves and our families and our situations, wondering why Carol doesn't do this and Paul doesn't do that. Or we can accept people as they are, faults included, and work to become what a happy family should be—a group of related people who are all good friends.

This book was written for you. But if your parents would like to read more about getting along in families, they might enjoy the following books:

Between Parent and Child by Haim G. Ginott: Macmillan, 1965.

Child Behavior by Frances L. Ilg, M.D. and Louse Bates Ames, Ph.D.: Harper & Row, 1965.

Children and Their Parents by Suzanne Strait Fremon: Harper & Row, 1968.

Dialogues With Mothers by Bruno Bettelheim: Macmillan, 1962.

The Family by Margaret Mead: Macmillan, 1965.

ABOUT THE AUTHOR

Even though her first story was published when she was sixteen, Phyllis Reynolds Naylor never planned a writing career. Her desire was to be a clinical psychologist. To earn money for studies at Washington University in the District of Columbia she wrote and published fiction stories. By the time she received her B.A. in psychology, Phyllis Naylor knew writing was her first love. Plans to go on to graduate school were dropped, and she began writing in earnest.

Mrs. Naylor writes at least six hours a day while her sons Jeffrey and Michael are in school. More than fifteen hundred of her articles and stories have been published in some two hundred magazines. *Getting Along in Your*

Family is Mrs. Naylor's twenty-third book for young readers.

The Naylors live in Bethesda, Maryland, where Mr. Naylor is chief of speech pathology at the Bethesda Naval Hospital.